Narrowboat Kitchen

Easy Recipes

More About My Life On A Narrowboat

By
Janul

Janul Publications

Published by Janul Publications

Copyright © 2011, Jan Knox

ISBN: 978-1-906921-07-1

Other books by the Author:

Lines From The Heart & Valentine Verses, 2009

The Adventures Of Pirate:
Through The Lock, 2010
Pirate In The Dock, 2010
Pirate Goes To A Festival, 2010

My Life On A Narrowboat, 2011

All copyrights Jan Knox
www.janulpublications.com / publications@janul.com

Contents

The Narrowboat Cooking Ethos ---------- 5

Pan Cooked Pleasures
- Beef Stew ---------------------- 7
- Scotch Broth ---------------------- 8
- Sausages, Onions & Mash ---------------------- 9
- Chilli Con Carne ---------------------- 10
- Easy Spaghetti Bolognese -------- 11
- Quick Economy Curry ---------------------- 12
- Savoury Omelette ---------------------- 13
- Liver & Onions ---------------------- 14
- Creamy Porridge ---------------------- 15

Oven Overtures
- Quick Chicken Pasta ---------------------- 17
- Lamb Bake ---------------------- 18
- Tommy's Sausage Plait ---------------------- 19
- Savoury Chicken Crumble -------- 20
- Shepherds Pie ---------------------- 21
- Chicken Chasseur ---------------------- 22
- Sunday Dinner Pie ---------------------- 23
- Cheese & Potato Pie ---------------------- 24
- Braised Steak In Red Wine or Ale -------- 25
- Classic Beef Lasagne ---------------------- 26
- Beef or Lamb Hotpot ---------------------- 27
- Stuffed Jacket Potatoes ---------------------- 28
- Cheesy Ciabatta ---------------------- 29

Proper Puddings
- Bread Pudding ---------------------- 31
- Fruit Crumble ---------------------- 32
- Jam Sponge ---------------------- 33

Perennial Preserves & Winter Warmers
- Blackberry Jam ---------------------- 35
- Damson Jam ---------------------- 36
- Sloe Gin ---------------------- 37
- Blackberry Vodka ---------------------- 38
- Jampot Jubbly ---------------------- 39

4

The Narrowboat Cooking Ethos

"Improvise because Instructions Won't Apply!"

Many of us live on narrowboats.
Many more use them for leisure or take holidays on them.

But some of us still travel with boatmen's cabins where food preparation always was & still is a matter of compromise.

So it will be little surprise to learn that this recipe book is a set of guidelines, not instructions, because the boatman's range remains the boss which can be persuaded into a happy working relationship - & you will love it.

Of course, those of you who aren't privy to the traditional narrowboat galley don't have to be deprived – the recipes work just as well with conventional cooking methods & you possibly have the happy advantage of being able to find what you need without walking miles along a muddy towpath.

Don't be put off by the approximate weights of food, alternative ingredients & the wide range of cooking temperatures which include "lower the heat, if you can" or "somewhere around xxx degrees", because these recipes & methods WORK.

I avoid most convenience meals but can appreciate the benefits of pre-prepared sauces which can be adapted to compliment traditional recipes when added to fresh ingredients.

Economy was part of my upbringing, so don't be alarmed at my use of leftovers which may save you money.

These recipes are the ones that I use every day.
I hope you enjoy them.

Janul

Pan Cooked Pleasures

Beef Stew
Warm & Waiting.

Ingredients (Serves 4):

500 grams cubed beef
2 large carrots
Stockpot jelly (or cube)
Salt & pepper to taste
Gravy powder or granules

1 large onion, peeled
2 large potatoes, peeled
Small can garden peas
Hot water
Splash of wine (optional)

Method:
Chop onion, carrots & potatoes. Place beef in a heavy based saucepan and cook in own fat until the meat is beginning to brown. Add vegetables & cook for a few minutes. If adding red wine, do this now. Cook for a further minute, add salt & pepper, then add the stockpot jelly, stirring well to combine. Add the garden peas & sufficient hot water to just cover the ingredients. Reduce heat (if possible!) & simmer for at least ½ hour. This can be left on low heat for hours, check it does not boil dry, adding more water as necessary. Mix gravy powder with a little water or use gravy granules & stir in well to form a thick stew.

Serve with crusty bread.

Note: *Beef can be replaced with chicken, just add a little sage.*

Scotch Broth
Economic & Tasty.

Ingredients (Serves 4):

Leftover lamb or lamb bone
2 large carrots
1/2 small swede
Stockpot jelly (or cube)
Hot water

1 medium onion, peeled
1/2 small cabbage
Handful pearl barley
Salt & pepper to taste

Method:
Chop onion, carrots, cabbage & swede finely. Place in a heavy based saucepan with pearl barley & cover with hot water. Add salt & pepper & the stockpot jelly, stirring well to combine. Place lamb bone on top of vegetables or stir in the leftover meat.

Bring to the boil & reduce heat until vegetables are very tender. This can be left on a low heat for hours, but check it does not boil dry. Add more water if necessary. If using lamb bone, strip meat from bone & replace in soup.

Serve with crusty bread.

Sausages, Mash & Onions
Energy Food For Lock Wheelers

Ingredients (Serves 4):
1.5 kilos floury potatoes, peeled & chopped
Knob of butter
Milk for mashing
Sausages (3 or 4 per person)
2 large onions, chopped

Method:
Place potatoes in a large saucepan, cover with salted water & boil until tender. Drain. Mash with the butter & a little milk.

Meanwhile, place sausages over low to medium heat in a large frying pan. Cook, turning frequently until golden brown.

Remove sausages from pan & keep warm whilst frying onions in some of the sausage fat.

Serve sausages around a central bed of mash & pile onions on top. Delicious when you add mushy peas or baked beans.

Chilli Con Carne
A true Mexican Favourite.

Ingredients (Serves 4):
500 grams minced beef
2 green peppers, cored
1 tin tomatoes
Extra chillies (optional)
Splash of red wine (optional)

1 large onion, peeled
2 tins red kidney beans (drained)
1 jar ready made chilli cooking sauce
Drizzle of cooking oil

Method:
Chop onion, peppers & chillies (if using). Using a large wok or heavy based saucepan, fry in the oil until starting to go soft. Add minced beef and cook until the meat is beginning to brown. If adding red wine, do this now.

Add the chilli sauce, tomatoes & kidney beans & when starting to bubble, cook for about 15 minutes (reducing heat where possible), stirring every few minutes to prevent sticking.

Serve with crusty bread or rice.

For improved flavour, let the pot go cold and reheat thoroughly before serving.

Easy Spaghetti Bolognese
For A Little Italian Flair

Ingredients (Serves 4):
500 grams minced beef
1 large onion, peeled & chopped
100 grams mushrooms, chopped
1 tin tomatoes
1 jar ready made Bolognese or tomato sauce
Splash of red wine (optional)
500 gram packet of dried spaghetti
Parmesan or other grated cheese to finish

Method:
Using a large wok or heavy based saucepan, fry the vegetables with the minced beef and cook until the meat is beginning to brown. If adding red wine, do this now.

Add the Bolognese sauce & tomatoes & when starting to bubble, cook for about 15 minutes (reducing heat where possible) & stirring every few minutes to prevent sticking).

Serve with spaghetti cooked as per instructions on packet. Garnish with parmesan or other grated cheese to finish. Serve with garlic bread and a green or mixed salad if available.

Quick Economy Curry
Waste not want not Indian Mystique

Ingredients (Serves 4):
Diced left over meat - lamb, beef, pork etc – whatever you have
1 large onion, peeled & chopped
Drizzle of oil
1 jar ready made Curry sauce, variety to taste (eg. Korma, madras)
2 cups of rice (standard coffee mugs will do!)

Method:
Using a large wok or heavy based saucepan, heat the oil & fry the meat with the onion until ingredients are beginning to brown.

Add the curry sauce & when starting to bubble, cook for about 10 minutes (reducing heat where possible) & stirring every few minutes to prevent sticking). Ensure that the meat is reheated thoroughly.

Serve with boiled rice which has been cooked as per packet instructions or use pre-prepared rice which is heated as directed by manufacturer.

Add puppodums & naan bread or chapatis as available in local towpath shops.

Savoury Omelette
Fast food on the move

Ingredients (Serves 1):

3 eggs
Knob of butter
25 grams grated strong cheese
Salt & pepper to taste

Method:
Whisk the eggs until frothy, adding salt & pepper.
Melt the butter in a small frying pan & swirl round the pan to evenly coat the base.

Add the egg mixture to the bubbling butter. As the eggs start to set, stir gently, smoothing the runny egg mixture over the surface to keep the omelette even. When almost set, sprinkle the cheese over the top.

Put under a hot grill (if one is available) until the cheese bubbles. If you do not have grilling facilities, fold the omelette in half so that the cheese melts in the middle as the egg sets.

Serve immediately accompanied with a green salad & crusty bread.

Note: *For more portions use a larger pan & triple the ingredients. Cooked meat or veg can be lightly fried before adding the eggs.*

Liver & Onions
Cheap & Cheerful

Ingredients (Serves 4):

Pig or sheep liver   Sliced onions
Gravy powder/granules   Drizzle of oil for frying

Method:
Fry chunks of liver (as much as you fancy or can afford) in the oil until sealed and turning brown on outside. Add onions & fry for a few minutes to soften.

Add hot water, enough to make gravy (lots or little as you like) and simmer for about 10-15 minutes to make sure the liver is cooked thoroughly. Add more water as necessary.

Thicken, using gravy powder & water or granules. Keep on low heat or cover & leave to stand.

Delicious with creamy mashed potatoes & lots of the gravy.

Note: If it's within your budget you can add bacon. Fry rashers to your liking in a separate pan & serve the bacon on top of the liver.

Creamy Porridge
For Inside Insulation

Ingredients (Serves 4):
12 dessertspoonfuls of oats
Knob butter
Single or double cream

500ml milk
Sugar to taste

Method:
Put oats, milk & butter in a saucepan & cook over a fairly low heat, stirring continuously to prevent sticking. Simmer, still stirring, for approx 5 minutes until thick & creamy.

Remove from heat.

Add sugar to taste & stir well.

Add single or double cream for a touch of indulgence.

Note: Can be cooked in a microwave in single portions. Cook for 90 seconds, in the serving bowl. Add sugar & cream after cooking, as above.

Oven Overtures

Quick Chicken Pasta
Cheat-time chic

Ingredients (Serves 4):
1 pack of cooked chopped chicken (or leftovers)
1 pack of fresh pasta shapes   Large jar white sauce
50 grams strong cheese   1/3 mug cold water

Method:
Place 2/3 of the white sauce into a jug and add 1/3 mug water to thin the sauce.

Cook pasta as directed on packet, drain & mix in 2/3 jar of white sauce, water & chicken. Place in ovenproof dish.

Pour the remaining white sauce onto the top of the pasta mixture & sprinkle the cheese over the top.

Place in oven until hot & the top is golden brown (somewhere between 170°-200° degrees, Gas mark 4-6 until done!).

Serve with salad and garlic bread or cheese ciabatta (page 29).

Note: *Leftover ham can be diced & used in the dish to bulk out the chicken & add extra flavour.*

Lamb Bake
Lamby Luxury

Ingredients (Serves 4):

500 grams minced lamb
100 grams Mushrooms
500 grams new potatoes
1 jar white sauce

1 large onion, peeled & chopped
Small carton passata
Splash of red wine (optional)
Parmesan or other grated cheese

Method:
Slice the new potatoes & boil in salted water until tender. Drain.

Meanwhile, using a large wok or heavy based saucepan, fry the onions & mushrooms with the minced lamb & cook until the meat is beginning to brown. If adding red wine, do this now. Add the passata & when starting to bubble, cook for about 5 minutes (reducing heat where possible) & stirring to prevent sticking). Place the meat mixture in the bottom of an ovenproof dish. Arrange the cooked potatoes over the meat then pour the white sauce over the top & sprinkle with cheese.

Place in oven until the top is golden brown (somewhere between 170°-200° degrees, Gas mark 4-6 until done!).

Serve with salad & garlic bread or cheese ciabatta (page 29).

Tommy's Sausage Plait
A Treat for the Tillerman

Ingredients (Serves 4):
500 grams good quality sausagemeat
Small onion, finely diced
Ready made puff pastry sheet
Marmite (optional)

Method:
Mix sausagemeat in a bowl with the diced onion.
Spread marmite (if using) on the pastry.
Pile the sausagemeat mixture evenly down the centre third of the pastry sheet.

Make equal slits in the pastry on either side of the meat, to form "fingers" which can be folded over to make the "plait".

Fold the pastry from alternate sides, forming the "plait".

Place on an ovenproof tray & place into the centre of a moderate oven. (About 170°-180°). Cook for about 50 minutes, ensuring that the sausage meat is cooked through.

Serve hot with baked beans & jacket potatoes.

Savoury Chicken Crumble
Store-cupboard Staple

Ingredients (Serves 4):

2 cans chicken in white sauce
50 grams granary flour
50 grams strong cheese

Tinned carrots & peas
30 grams butter

Method:
Place canned chicken in white sauce in an ovenproof dish. Drain the canned vegetables (or use left over vegetables) & gently mix into the chicken mixture – take care not to squash the vegetables.

In a mixing bowl, rub together the flour and butter to make a crumble. Stir in the cheese and sprinkle the crumble mixture lightly over the chicken.

Bake in a fairly hot oven (180° - 200°C /Gas mark 5-6) for 30-45 minutes until the crumble is turning brown.

Serve with sweetcorn, green beans & warm bread.

Shepherds Pie
A Classic Comfort

Ingredients (Serves 4):

500 grams minced beef
Stockpot jelly (or cube)
Gravy powder or granules
25 grams butter

1 medium onion, peeled & chopped
Splash of red wine (optional)
1 kilo potatoes

Method:

Peel & chop the potatoes. Boil in salted water until tender. Drain and mash with the butter.

Whilst potatoes are boiling, fry the onions with the minced beef & cook until the meat is beginning to brown. If adding red wine, do this now. Add the stockpot jelly & water (about 1/2 mug). When bubbling, gradually add gravy powder (about a dessertspoonful) which has been mixed with a little cold water, stirring constantly. Cook for a further 5 minutes, turning down the heat (if possible), stirring every few minutes to prevent sticking).
Place the meat mixture in an ovenproof dish and pile the mashed potatoes on top, coating evenly & fluffing up with a fork.

Place in oven until the top is golden brown (somewhere between 170°-200° degrees, Gas mark 4-6 until done!).

Chicken Chasseur
Posh Chicken Casserole

Ingredients (Serves 4):

4 chicken portions
2 large carrots, chopped
1 jar chasseur sauce
Splash of oil

Medium Onion, peeled & chopped
200 gram button mushrooms, whole
Splash sherry (optional)

Method:
Heat oil in heavy based frying pan and brown the chicken breasts to seal. Put in a casserole dish with lid or use a slow cooker.

Add vegetables to the frying pan and cook for a few minutes to absorb any chicken juices from the pan. Add the sherry if using, then the ready made chasseur sauce.

Pour the sauce mixture over the chicken, cover & cook in the oven (180 degrees C or Gas Mark 5 are ideal) for about 90 minutes or until the chicken and vegetables are thoroughly cooked.

If using a slow cooker the dish will take about 6-8 hours to cook.

Serve with mashed potatoes & green vegetables.

Sunday Dinner Pie
Leftovers In A Blanket

Ingredients (Serves 4):
Leftover meat
Leftover vegetables, including potatoes
Leftover gravy or gravy powder/granule gravy
Sheet of ready made puff pastry

Method:
Place meat, vegetables & gravy in an ovenproof dish.

Cover with pastry lid & seal the edges to the dish with a little water. Cut sits in the top of the pie for steam to escape.

Place in centre of moderate oven until the pastry is cooked through all the layers & is golden brown (180 degrees C or Gas Mark 5 are ideal). This will take about 45 minutes to 1 hour.

Serve with crusty bread & extra gravy if you have any.

Note: After a hard day travelling this is delicious followed by a proper pudding to set you up for the next day.

Cheese & Potato Pie
Comforting Melt After A Storm

Ingredients (Serves 4):
1.5 kilos floury potatoes, peeled & chopped
200 grams grated strong cheese
50 grams small cubed strong cheese
Knob of butter
Salt & pepper to taste

Method:
Place potatoes in a large saucepan, cover with salted water & boil until tender. Drain.

Mash potatoes, stir in the butter & all but a little of the grated cheese. Place mixture in an ovenproof dish.
Press cubes of cheese into the surface of the potatoes in symmetrical pattern. Finish by sprinkling remaining grated cheese on the top of the potatoes.

Place in oven until the top is golden brown (somewhere between 160-200 degrees, Gas mark 4-6 until done!).

Serve with baked beans & crusty bread.
Can also be used as a side dish for sausages or chops.

Braised Steak In Red Wine or Ale
Rich & Red for cold evenings.

Ingredients (Serves 4):
4 cheap cut steaks
1 small green pepper, cored
200 grams button mushrooms
1 medium onion peeled & chopped
1 jar or can of red wine or ale cooking sauce
Splash of wine or ale (optional)

Method:
In a large, heavy frying pan, seal the steaks over a high heat. Place in a covered casserole dish or slow cooker.
Fry the pepper, mushrooms & onion in the steak juices for a few minutes until the vegetables start to soften. If using wine or ale, add it now & cook for a minute or 2 before adding the cooking sauce to the pan. Heat through & pour over the steaks.

Oven cook (170°-190° C or Gas Mark 5-6) for about 90 minutes. If using a slow cooker the dish will take about 6-8 hours to cook.

Serve with jacket potatoes & seasonal vegetables.

Note: *Chicken can be used with red wine sauce for "Coq au Vin".*

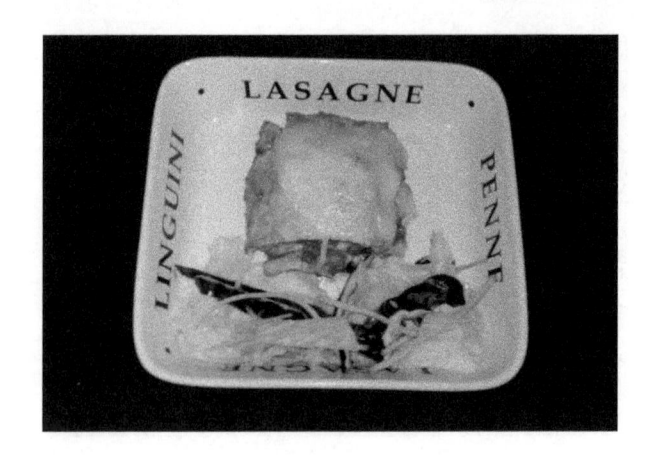

Classic Beef Lasagne
A Firm Favourite

Ingredients (Serves 4):

500 grams minced beef
1 tin tomatoes
1 pack fresh lasagne sheets
1 jar white sauce

1 large onion, peeled & chopped
1 jar ready made tomato based sauce
Splash of red wine (optional)
Parmesan or other grated cheese

Method:
Using a large wok or heavy based saucepan, fry the onions with the minced beef & cook until the meat is beginning to brown. If adding red wine, do this now. Add the tomato based sauce & tinned tomatoes & when starting to bubble, cook for about 10 minutes (reducing heat where possible) & stirring every few minutes to prevent sticking).

Divide the lasagne sheets into 3 & layer the meat sauce evenly between the sheets, starting with the sauce & finishing with pasta. Pour white sauce onto the top of the lasagne & sprinkle cheese over the top.
Place in oven until hot & the top is golden brown (somewhere between 170°-200° degrees, Gas mark 4-6 until done!).

Serve with salad & garlic bread or cheese ciabatta (page 29).

Beef or Lamb Hotpot
Hot & Hearty

Ingredients (Serves 4):
500 grams minced beef or lamb
1 kilo potatoes, peeled & sliced
1 large onion, peeled & chopped

Carrots, chopped
Frozen or tinned peas
Stock jelly or cube

Method:
Put mince into a large ovenproof dish or casserole. Add stock jelly/cube, carrots, onions & peas (no need to pre-cook veg). Stir in hot water so that stock dissolves.

Arrange raw sliced potatoes on top of the dish. Add enough water to the dish to cover the potatoes – this will reduce during cooking.

Place in oven between 170°-200° degrees, Gas Mark 4-6 until the liquid has reduced & the potatoes start to go crispy. This will take a couple of hours (more or less, depending on your oven facilities!) Make sure the bottom of the dish does not boil dry, add more hot water as necessary to prevent from burning.

Serve with hot bread to mop up the broth.

Stuffed Jacket Potatoes
Leftover Warmth

Ingredients (Serves 4):
4 large jacket potatoes
200 grams grated strong cheese
Leftover meat, finely cubed
Salt & pepper to taste

Method:
Cook potatoes in their jackets. This can be done by using the oven if it is on (an advantage if the boatman's galley stove is alight) or microwave, until a knife can be passed through the potatoes. Prick the potato skins before putting in either type of oven.

Allow to cool a little, cut each potato in half & scoop potato flesh into a bowl. Mash with most of the cheese, then mix in the leftover meat. Pile the mixture back into the skins and place in the oven until the tops of the potatoes are golden brown (somewhere between 160-200 degrees, Gas mark 4-6 until done!).

Serve with baked beans.

Can also be used as an accompaniment for other dishes.

Cheesy Ciabatta
Delicious for dipping

Ingredients (Serves 4):
1 large or 4 small ciabattas (fresh or long life part-baked)
200 grams grated strong cheese
Butter

Method:
Slice the ciabatta lengthways (to separate top & bottom).

Butter both halves of the loaf generously.

Place grated cheese on the bottom layer & sandwich the layers together.

Wrap in foil and place in the oven (160-200 degrees, Gas mark 4-6) for about 10 minutes. Check & if the cheese is melting, remove the foil & place back in the oven until the loaf starts to crisp.

Serve hot as an accompaniment for other dishes.

Note: *Leftover French stick or other bread can also be used for economy. If bread is going stale, sprinkle with a little cold water to re-hydrate when cooking.*

Proper Puddings

Bread Pudding
An old fashioned favourite.

Ingredients (Serves 4):
1/2 loaf of white bread, preferably stale, crusts cut off
50 grams suet   150 grams sugar
1 egg   50 grams sultanas or currants
Boiling water

Method:
In a large bowl, break the bread into small pieces. Add boiling water sparingly, a little at a time, beating until the bread resembles a smooth pulp.

Add the egg, suet, sugar & sultanas, mixing well until combined.

Turn into a small ovenproof dish & oven cook (170°-190° C or Gas Mark 5-6) until golden brown on top.

Remove from oven & immediately sprinkle with sugar.

Can be served hot or cold.

This is delicious when served warm with cream or custard.

Fruit Crumble
Fruity Foraging.

Ingredients (Serves 4):
Seasonal Fruit & sugar to taste or canned fruit filling
150 grams plain flour   75 grams margarine
75 grams sugar   (Or packet crumble mix)

Method:
Prepare seasonal fruit such as blackberries (remove leaves & wash), damsons or plums (wash, split & remove stones) or apples (peel, core & slice). Put in an ovenproof dish & add sugar to taste.

In a large bowl, rub the flour & margarine together with your fingers until it resembles crumble. Stir in the sugar. (Or use the packet crumble mix).

Spread the crumble mixture over the prepared fruit, or the canned fruit filling if using. Oven cook (170°-190° C or Gas Mark 5-6) until golden brown on top.

Serve warm with cream or custard.

Note: *Don't forget to forage for fruits on the towpath – but only eat them if you're sure what they are!*

Sponge Pudding
Calorific Comfort

Ingredients (Serves 4):

100 grams margarine   200 grams self raising flour
1 egg   100 grams sugar
1 tablespoon milk   2 tablespoons Jam or golden syrup

Method:
Beat the margarine and the sugar together until light & fluffy. Beat the egg separately & add slowly to the sponge mixture. Add the milk gradually until mixture forms a dropping consistency from a wooden spoon.

Grease a large pudding basin or 4 individual basins & put jam or golden syrup into the bottom. Pour the sponge mixture on top.

Cover with foil & steam for about 90 minutes or oven cook for about 40 minutes (170°-190° C or Gas Mark 5-6) until risen & until a knife comes out clean when placed in centre of sponge.

Alternatively, microwave for 4 minutes for a large pudding (times may vary with oven).

Turn out onto a plate & serve with custard or cream.

Perennial Preserves & Winter Warmers

Blackberry Jam
Best of British

Ingredients
Blackberries – best picked wild from hedgerows. Weigh them.
Granulated sugar – use the same amount of sugar as fruit
Knob of butter

Method:
Wash blackberries & remove any bits of twig, hedgerow etc.
In a large, heavy saucepan, put blackberries with butter & start to heat. Add sugar gradually, stirring continually to prevent sticking. Increase heat if possible & keep stirring until mixture reaches a rolling boil (boils frantically!). Reduce heat if possible. Gradually the froth on top of the pan will lessen & the jam will start to thicken slightly & turn darker. This happens from 5 minutes but can take much longer depending on the amount of pectin (setting agent) in fruit. Test for "setting point" by placing a teaspoon of the mixture onto a clean saucer. Leave for 1 minute. When it is "done", the jam will wrinkle when pushed, ie "set".
For blackberry jelly (optional), pass through a sieve to strain out pips (this can be put aside for "Jampot Jubbly"!).
Pour into warm jars & seal with airtight lids just before cold.

Keep in fridge or in cool place below the water line of your boat.

Damson Jam
For Foraging Flavour

Ingredients
Damsons – best picked wild from the towpath. Weigh them.
Granulated sugar – use the same amount of sugar as fruit
Knob of butter

Method:
Wash damsons & remove any bits of twig, hedgerow etc. Split each damson carefully with a sharp knife to make cooking quicker. Follow recipe as for blackberry jam, until testing for setting point.

Test for "setting point" by placing a teaspoon of the mixture onto a clean saucer. Leave for 1 minute. When it is "done", the jam will wrinkle when pushed, ie "set".

Pass through a colander to strain out stones & skin (this can be put aside for "Jampot Jubbly"). Pour into warm jars & seal with airtight lids just before cold.

Delicious served with hot buttered toast or with buttered scones.

Keep in fridge or in cool place below the water line of your boat.

Sloe Gin
Ready for Christmas – for adults only!

Ingredients
Sloes – no exact science here, fill about 1/3 of an airtight jar
Granulated sugar – use the same amount of sugar as fruit
Gin

Method:
Wash sloes & remove any twigs or debris. If making immediately, prick each sloe with a knitting needle to release juice. If you are in no hurry & have a freezer, freeze the sloes & when they defrost they will have split, saving time & effort.

Place sloes in an airtight jar or pot. Add about the same amount of sugar. Top up with gin.

Give the jar a good shake so that the fruit, sugar & gin are well combined. This does take a bit of effort at first! Repeat daily for a couple of months.

Strain the mixture through a sieve to remove large pieces of fruit. Allow to settle & "rack" the liquid a couple of times over a month to pour the sloe gin into a clean container & away from the sediment.

Blackberry Vodka
Berry Nice – for adults only!

Ingredients
Blackberries – no exact science here, fill about 1/3 of the jar
Granulated sugar – use the same amount of sugar as fruit
Vodka

Method:
Wash blackberries & remove any twigs or debris. Place in an airtight jar or pot. Add about the same amount of sugar. Top up with vodka.

Give the jar a good shake so that the fruit, sugar & vodka are well combined. This does take a bit of effort at first! Repeat daily for a couple of months.

Strain the mixture through a sieve to remove large pieces of fruit. Allow to settle & "rack" the liquid a couple of times over a month to pour the vodka into a clean container & away from the sediment.

Enjoy!

Jampot Jubbly
Waste Not Want More – for adults only!

Ingredients
The stones, pips & skin mixture strained from making jam (sticky!)
Gin, Vodka, brandy or rum to taste!

Method:
Spoon the jampot remains into an airtight jar or wide necked bottle. Top up with alcohol of your choice.

Damson, blackberry, raspberry & strawberry go well with gin or vodka. Plum goes well with brandy. Be inventive with what you have, it's part of the fun!

Give the jar a good shake so that the fruit "jubbly" & alcohol are well combined. Repeat daily for a couple of months.

Strain the mixture through a sieve to remove stones & skin. Allow to settle & "rack" the liquid a couple of times over a month to pour the jubbly into a clean container & away from the sediment. This does take patience for the clearing process & may remain cloudy.

Drink sparingly!

Dedicated to Warren,
"Storm" & "Pirate"

Also dedicated to Bill Buckley, my Dad, who inspired me through his memories of growing up in wartime Britain

Acknowledgement to Tom Hill for "Tommy's Sausage Plait"

Lightning Source UK Ltd.
Milton Keynes UK
UKHW021059170520
363414UK00002B/326